W9-DBH-322

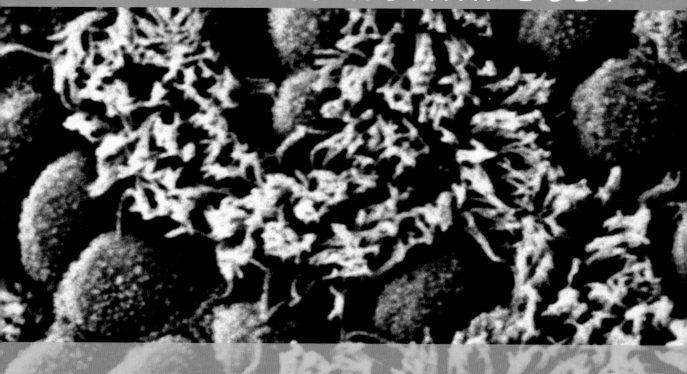

RESPIRATORY SYSTEM

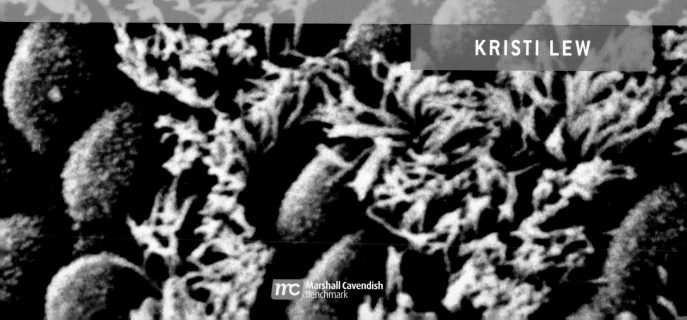

KRISTI LEW

mc Marshall Cavendish
Benchmark

Marshall Cavendish Benchmark

99 White Plains Road

Tarrytown, New York 10591

www.marshallcavendish.us

Editor: Karen Ang

Publisher: Michelle Bisson

Art Director: Anahid Hamparian

Series Design by: Kay Petronio

Series Designer: Elynn Cohen

Library of Congress Cataloging-in-Publication Data

Lew, Kristi.

Respiratory system / by Kristi Lew.

p. cm. -- (The amazing human body)

Includes bibliographical references and index.

Summary: "Discusses the parts that make up the human respiratory system, what can go wrong, how to treat those
illnesses and diseases, and how to stay healthy"--Provided by publisher.

ISBN 978-0-7614-4042-0

1. Respiratory organs--Juvenile literature. 2. Respiration--Juvenile literature. I. Title.

QP121.L49 2010   612.2--dc22   2008037269

 = alveoli in the lungs

Front cover: An X ray of the lungs   Title page: The surface of the trachea   Back Cover: The branches of the bronchial tree

Photo research by Tracey Engel

Front cover photo: Barts Hospital / Getty

The photographs in this book are used by permission and through the courtesy of: Getty Images: Dave King, 67, back
cover; Dorling Kindersly, 4; 3D4Medical.com, 8, 27, 36, 47; Kallista Images, 9; Nucleus Medical Art, Inc., 12, 19, 44 (top and
bottom); 3D Clinic, 20, 26, 31, 51, 63; Ralph Hutchings, 22, 56; Dr. David M. Phillips, 25; Dr. Don Fawcett, 29; Yellow Dog
Productions, 33; S. Lowry/Univ Uster, 38; RMF, 41; Bruce Ayres, 46; Beto Hacker, 54; SMC Images, 57; Gazimal, 58; Steven
Puetzer, 65; Chris Cole, 66; Romilly Lockyer, 70. Alamy: Nucleus Medical Art, Inc., 10, 42, 49, 52, 59, 62; Image Source Pink,
16; MedicalRF.com, 18; Design Pics, Inc., 30; Corbis Premium RF, 50; Carol Donner / PHOTOTAKE, 64; BSIP / PHOTOTAKE, 71.
Photo Researchers, Inc.: BSIP, 6, 14 (top and bottom), 69; Eye of Science, 7; Christian Darkin, 11; Dr. P. Marazzi, 15; Steve
Gschmeissner, 34; Brian Evans, 39. SuperStock: Image Source, 1, 28, 43.

Printed in Malaysia

123456

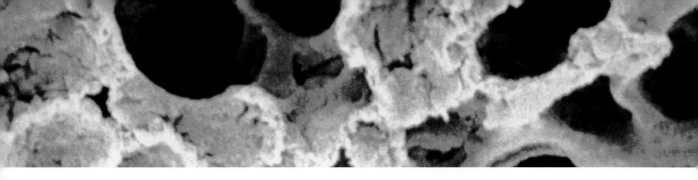

CONTENTS

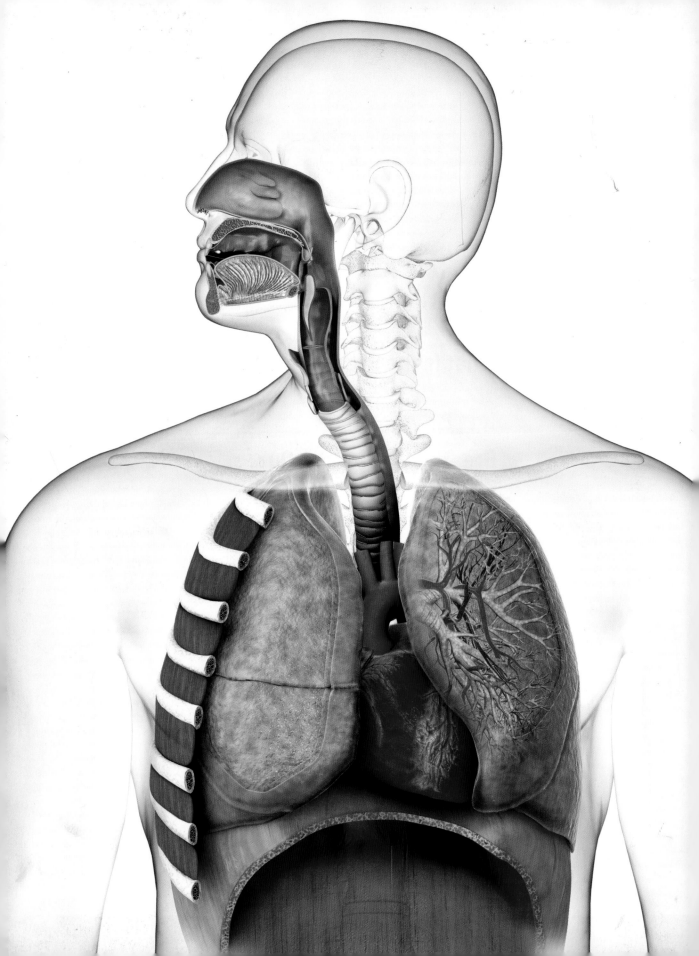

1

What Is the Respiratory System?

When most people think of the respiratory system, they naturally focus on the lungs and breathing. Indeed, breathing is a necessary function of a healthy body. Without the lungs taking in air, the cells of the body could not operate properly. However, the lungs are only one part of the respiratory system. The respiratory system also includes the nose, mouth, pharynx, larynx (voice box), trachea (windpipe), bronchi, alveoli, and diaphragm.

The airways of the body are commonly divided into two sections by the medical profession—the upper respiratory tract and the lower respiratory tract. The nose, pharynx, and larynx are considered the upper respiratory tract. The trachea, bronchial tree, and the lungs make up the lower respiratory tract.

The human respiratory system is made up of many different tissues and organs that work together to help us breathe.

THE NOSE AND MOUTH

In order to breathe, the body must take in air through the nose or mouth (also known as the oral cavity). Air is made up of many different gases. About 78 percent of it is nitrogen, 21 percent is oxygen, and argon, carbon dioxide, methane, and other more rare gases make up the last 1 percent. Of all the gases that make up the air we breathe, however, oxygen is the only one that the body can use.

The Nose

When air is taken in though the nose, it comes in through two holes called the nostrils, or external nares. Most of the respiratory system, including the nose, is lined with mucous membranes. Mucous membranes secrete a clear, thin, slippery fluid called mucus. Mucus traps small particles such as dust, viruses, and bacteria, preventing them from reaching the lungs. Small, stiff hairs in the nose also help to filter the air and keep pollen, insects, and other foreign particles out of the lungs. Along with filtering the air, the nose also moistens and warms the air taken in.

When people say their sinuses are bothering them, they

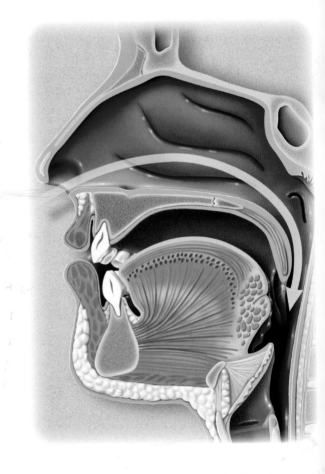

The soft tissues and membranes that line the nose allow air to be warmed, moistened, and filtered as it is inhaled.

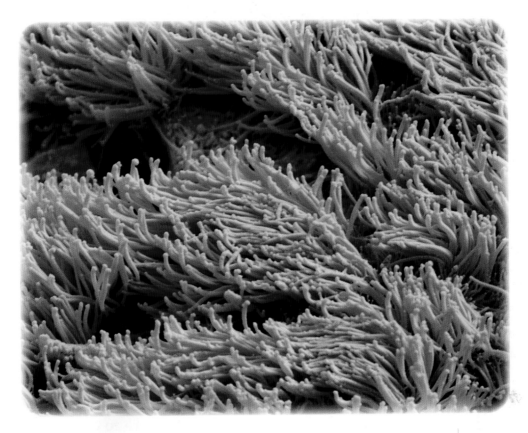

Microscopic hairs called cilia line the nasal passages. These hairs help to catch dust, dirt, and other foreign particles that can clog or infect the respiratory system.

are talking about the air-filled hollow spaces in the skull. These bony cavities lie on either side of the nose. The sinuses are lined with mucous membranes and open into the nasal passages. The mucus in the sinus cavities drains into the nose. If these passages get blocked and mucus cannot drain properly, the sinuses can get plugged with mucus. When this happens, it often results in a stuffy nose and a build up of pressure within the sinuses. The pressure often causes a painful sinus headache.

One thing that can prevent the sinuses from draining correctly is a deviated septum. The septum is the thin piece of tissue in the nose that separates the two nostrils. The front part of the septum is made of cartilage and is flexible. Further back, toward the skull, the septum is

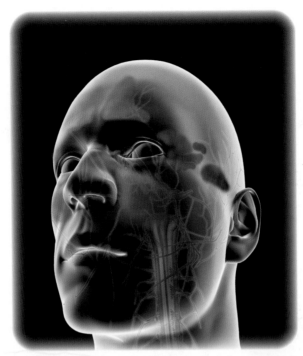

The red areas in this illustration show the locations of the sinuses.

made up of bone. When someone breaks their nose, they crack the bone of the septum. A deviated septum is one that lies more to one side of the nose than the other. About 80 percent of people have a deviated septum. Sometimes a person is born with a deviated septum, other times the deviation is a result of an injury to the nose. If the deviation is severe, it can affect the way the sinuses drain or cause a blockage in one of the nasal passages. This can cause a stuffy nose, frequent sinus infections, and nosebleeds. Some medication can help relieve some of the symptoms of a deviated septum, but surgery is required to correct it.

The Mouth

Most people breathe though their noses if they can. But sometimes, like when they have a cold and, therefore, a stuffy nose, people are forced to breathe through their mouths. This can cause several problems. Breathing through the mouth can cause a sore throat because the air is not moistened

SNEEZING

Most of the mucus produced by the nose travels down the throat—through passages connecting the nose to the throat—and is swallowed. Any foreign particles trapped in the mucus are usually destroyed by acid in the stomach. However, if too many particles build up in the mucus in the nose, they can irritate the mucus membranes. As a result, the nerve endings underneath the membranes trigger a sneezing reflex. The blast of air expelled through the nose during a sneeze is the body's way of sweeping the nasal passages clean.

The force of a sneeze drives saliva, mucus, and particles—such as dirt and germs—out of the respiratory system. Because the substances coming out of your nose and mouth can make others sick, you should always use a tissue when sneezing and coughing.

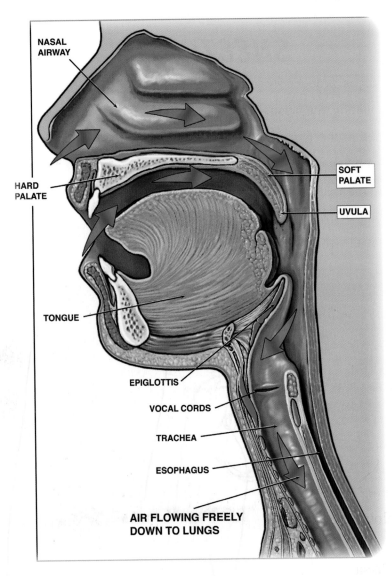

An illustration of the upper respiratory system shows how air can travel through the different passageways.

Labels on the illustration:
- NASAL AIRWAY
- SOFT PALATE
- UVULA
- HARD PALATE
- TONGUE
- EPIGLOTTIS
- VOCAL CORDS
- TRACHEA
- ESOPHAGUS
- AIR FLOWING FREELY DOWN TO LUNGS

as it is when it comes in through the nose. Air coming into the mouth does not get filtered as it does when it comes through the nose. This can lead to a respiratory infection if bacteria or viruses come in through the mouth. It can also cause damage to the lungs if dust, insects, or other foreign matter is inhaled. The body tries to protect the lungs from inhaling foreign objects with the cough reflex. Much like sneezing, coughing forcefully expels foreign particles from the body.

THE PHARYNX

The nose and mouth lead to a passageway called the pharynx. The pharynx is the scientific name for what most people call the throat. This passageway is shared by the respiratory and the digestive systems. The pharynx receives air from the nose and mouth to allow the respiratory system to do its work. It also accepts food and water from the mouth for the digestive system.

Just below the oral cavity, the pharynx splits into two passages—the esophagus and the trachea. The esophagus takes food from the mouth into the stomach. The trachea, or windpipe, diverts air from the nose and mouth to the

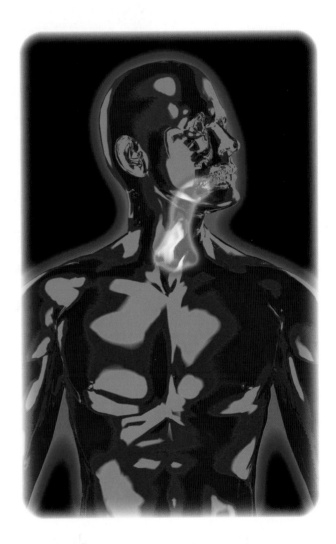

The pharynx, highlighted here in red, is more commonly called the throat.

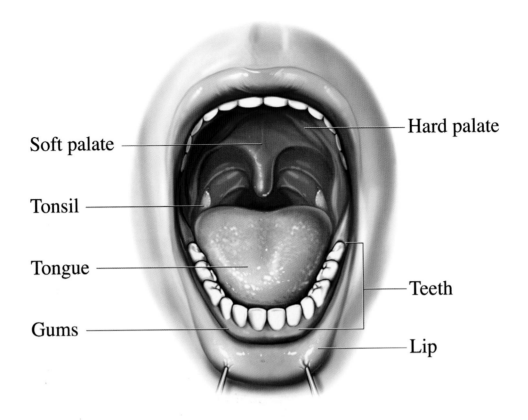

Soft palate

Hard palate

Tonsil

Tongue

Teeth

Gums

Lip

Uvulas can come in different shapes and sizes, depending upon how the hard and soft palate develop.

lungs. To prevent food from going down the trachea, a flap of tissue, called the epiglottis, covers the opening of the trachea during swallowing.

The Uvula

If you open your mouth wide, stick out your tongue, and look in a mirror, you will see a cylindrical-shaped piece of tissue hanging from the roof of your mouth in the back of your throat. This bit of tissue is called the uvula. The uvula forms when the two halves of the palate (the roof of the mouth) fuse together when you are developing as a fetus inside your mother.

No one knows for sure what the uvula's purpose may be. Some scientists think it may help with breathing, digestive processes, or even speech. Because of the way it forms, the uvula can have different appearances in different people. In most people, it looks like a solid tube

CLEFT PALATES

A completely unfused uvula is often the result of a cleft palate. The palate is the soft tissue (soft palate) and bone (hard palate) that make up the roof of the mouth. A cleft is a split or a crack between the two halves. A cleft results when one, or both, of these palates does not fuse correctly before a baby is born. A cleft lip is a narrow gap in the tissue between the upper lip and the bottom of the nose. A cleft palate is an opening in the roof of the mouth between the mouth and the nasal cavities.

Doctors are not certain exactly what causes the palates of babies born with clefts not to fuse. They believe that there is a genetic, or inherited, component to the condition because children who have siblings, parents, or other family members born with clefts have a higher risk of having a cleft, too. Scientists also think that factors in the environment, such as certain drugs, illnesses, or the use of tobacco or alcohol during pregnancy, also increase the risk of the birth defect. In the United States, about one in 1,000 babies are born with a cleft lip, cleft palate, or both. In fact, cleft lips and cleft palates are one of the most common major birth defects in America. A child with a cleft lip or palate may have trouble breathing, eating, and speaking. But doctors can now repair cleft lips and palates. Most children born with clefts have surgery to correct the condition within their first year or two of life.

of tissue. But some people's uvulas have a groove down one side. This groove results if the tissue does not completely fuse during development. A rarer uvula shape is the result of a partially unfused uvula. When this occurs, the uvula looks like an upside-down "Y." Even rarer is a completely unfused uvula that looks like two separate strips of tissue hanging down in the back of the throat.

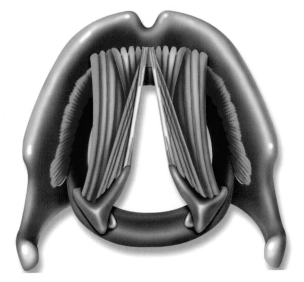

THE LARYNX

Sitting below the pharynx and on top of the trachea is a structure called the larynx, or the voice box. When people speak, parts of the larynx, called the vocal cords, vibrate as air is expelled from the lungs and rushes over them. This produces sound.

The vocal cords are two bands of elastic, smooth muscle tissue that are attached at the front and back of the throat. When we breathe in or out

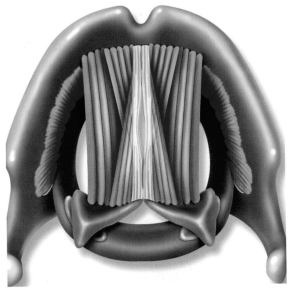

The sounds we make come from vibrations created when air moves the vocal cords.

ADENOIDS AND TONSILS

The adenoids and tonsils are tissues that lie at the top and sides of the throat. They are actually a part of the lymphatic and immune systems. The lymphatic system consists of lymph nodes, which are clusters or knots of cells, and lymph vessels (similar to blood vessels) that carry fluid throughout the body. The lymphatic system assists the immune system by filtering out foreign matter, including bacteria and viruses, which can cause infection. The lymphatic system also produces cells called lymphocytes that fight infection.

The adenoids are lymphatic tissue at the top of the throat. The tonsils are lymph nodes along the sides. Both are part of the infection-fighting system, but sometimes they get infected and swell. If medication does not reduce the swelling they may have to be removed. Because the body has other lymph nodes and lymphatic tissue to help fight infection, people can lead normal lives without adenoids or tonsils.

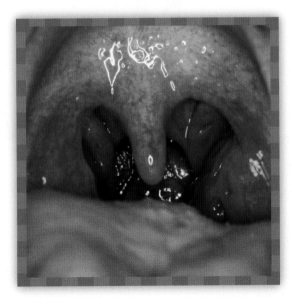

The tonsils are the round reddish objects at the back of the throat, on either side of the uvula. This photograph shows a pair of healthy tonsils.

without making any sounds, the vocal cords are open and do not touch. This allows air to move through the gap between the cords. This gap is called the glottis.

Making Sounds

To produce sound, the vocal cords must close. When the vocal cords are closed, they provide resistance to the air being exhaled from the lungs. When enough air pressure builds up, the vocal cords are "blown" apart. As air travels quickly through the vocal cords, the cords are sucked back together again. The vocal cords being blown apart and sucked back together again causes vibrations. The vibrations create sound. This movement of the vocal cords can occur hundreds or thousands of times a second. Muscular contractions in the throat, jaw, palate, lips, and tongue are required to shape the sound produced by the larynx into speech.

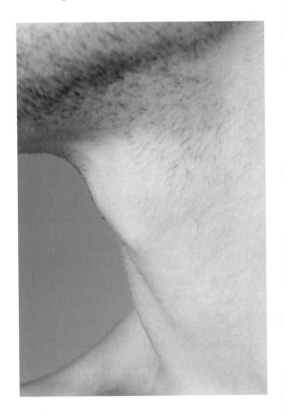

The pitch of a person's voice—whether the voice has a high-pitched, squeaky sound or is a low-pitched growl, for example—depends partially on the shape and tension of the vocal cords and partially on the shape of the person's nose, mouth, and throat. During puberty, the period when children undergo changes into adulthood, the larynx grows larger. In boys, the larynx grows large enough to stick out in the front of the throat. This bump is commonly called the Adam's

Men develop Adam's apples after they go through puberty. The size and shape of an Adam's apple can vary from person to person.

apple. Because adult males usually have a larger larynx, their vocal cords are longer than those in adult females or in children. This additional length produces a lower pitched voice.

The nose, mouth, and throat act as resonating chambers for the voice. Changing the shape of these resonating cavities, by removing the adenoids, for example, can change the sound of a person's voice. This is why some surgeons are reluctant to operate to remove adenoids or repair a deviated septum, for example, on a professional singer. These types of operations would change the shape of the singer's mouth or nose and possibly change the sound of the voice.

THE TRACHEA AND BRONCHI

Below the larynx is the trachea, or the windpipe. The trachea is the major airway for the body and it is made up of hard cartilage. The cartilage stiffens the trachea and prevents the pipe from collapsing in on itself. This hard cartilage can be felt in the front of the neck. The esophagus is behind the trachea. It is made of soft tissue and cannot be felt through the skin.

Like the nose, the trachea is lined with mucous membranes. The mucus in the trachea traps any foreign particles that get past the mucus and hairs in the nose. This mucus, or phlegm, is moved up into the throat where it is either expelled out of the body by coughing or swallowed. Any foreign particles swallowed with the phlegm are usually destroyed by stomach acids.

Partway down the chest, the trachea splits into two branches—the left and the right bronchi. These two branches feed air into the left and the right lung. The bronchial tubes are also lined with mucous membranes and with microscopic hair-like structures called cilia. The cilia move in tiny wavelike motions that move mucus up and out of the bronchi before it can get into the lungs.

THE LUNGS

The left and the right bronchi branch into smaller airways called the bronchioles. Each bronchiole ends in tiny, spongy sacs called alveoli. Each individual sac is called an alveolus. An average adult has more than 600 million alveoli. When a person inhales (breathes in) every alveolus fills with air. All together, the bronchi, bronchioles, and alveoli make up the bronchial tree.

The alveoli are surrounded by tiny blood vessels called capillaries. When a person inhales air, the oxygen in the air can move through the thin walls of the alveoli into the capillaries. Blood vessels then distribute the oxygen to the body. Carbon dioxide, a waste product that is carried

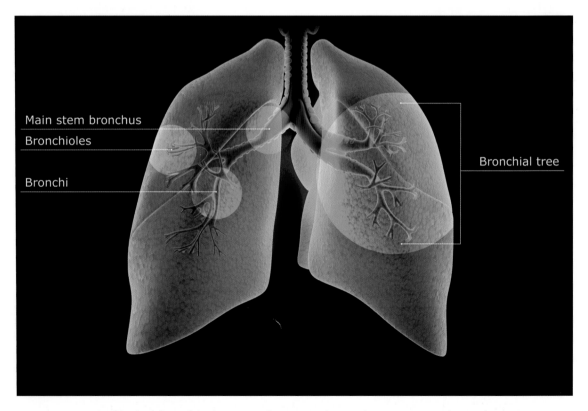

Main stem bronchus
Bronchioles

Bronchi

Bronchial tree

Inside the lobes of the lungs are the many tubes and passageways that make up the bronchial tree.

from other parts of the body through the blood vessels, can move through the capillary walls into the alveoli so that it can be exhaled.

In most people, the right lung is shorter and wider than the left and can hold a higher volume of air. The right lung has three sections, called lobes. The left lung is longer and skinnier. It has two lobes. The left lung also has an indentation in it called the cardiac notch. The top of the heart fits into the cardiac notch of the left lung. The lungs are both encased in a double membrane called the pleura. The two layers of tissue that make up the pleura are separated by a small amount of fluid. The pleura protects and cushions the lungs. The space in the chest that encases the lungs is called the pleural cavity.

Healthy alveoli look like little sacs surrounded by blood vessels.

THE DIAPHRAGM

The diaphragm is a sheet of strong muscle that lies at the bottom of the pleural cavity. It separates the chest cavity from the abdominal cavity. The diaphragm is actually a part of the muscular system. But the diaphragm is also absolutely necessary to the respiratory system.

During inhalation, the diaphragm contracts and pulls down. Muscles between the ribs, called the intercostals, also contract to pull

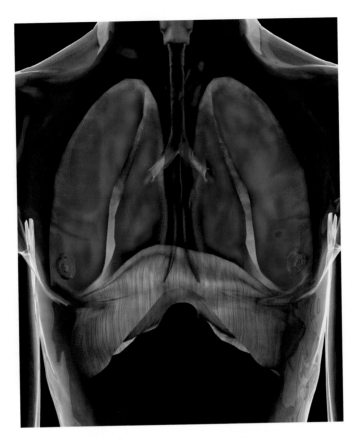

The diaphragm (beige) sits below the lungs (blue) and helps them inflate and deflate.

the ribs up and out slightly. This causes the chest cavity to become larger and increase in volume. This increase in volume causes air to flow into the lungs.

During exhalation, the opposite happens. The diaphragm and intercostals relax. The diaphragm moves upward and the ribs move in and down, forcing air (or, more specifically, carbon dioxide) out of the lungs. One full cycle of inhalation and exhalation is one breath. Average, normal adults take about twelve to fifteen breaths every minute.

The muscular system is not the only body system that helps the respiratory system do its job. The circulatory and nervous systems must also work closely with the lungs to get the body's cells the oxygen they need to function properly. Every three to five seconds, nerves tell the diaphragm to contract so that the body inhales. Exhaling is equally important. It releases carbon dioxide, a waste product that would poison the body's cells if it were not removed from the body. This exchange of necessary gases would not be possible without all of the organs in the respiratory system.

HICCUPS

Hiccups are caused by an involuntary spasm, or contraction, in the diaphragm. The diaphragm contracts suddenly causing air to be sucked into the throat. The vocal cords clamp shut just at the contraction begins and cause the "hic" sound.

Some things that may irritate the diaphragm and cause it to spasm are eating or drinking too quickly and feeling nervous or excited. Even sneezing or coughing can sometimes cause a case of the hiccups. But sometimes there is no specific cause. They just start up on their own for no apparent reason.

Hiccups can be annoying, but they are usually harmless and go away on their own. That does not stop people from trying to get them to leave quickly, however. Some common hiccup cures include holding your breath, drinking water, and having someone jump out and scare you. Most of these techniques rely on resetting a person's breathing pattern in an effort to start the diaphragm back on a regular schedule of contraction and relaxation.

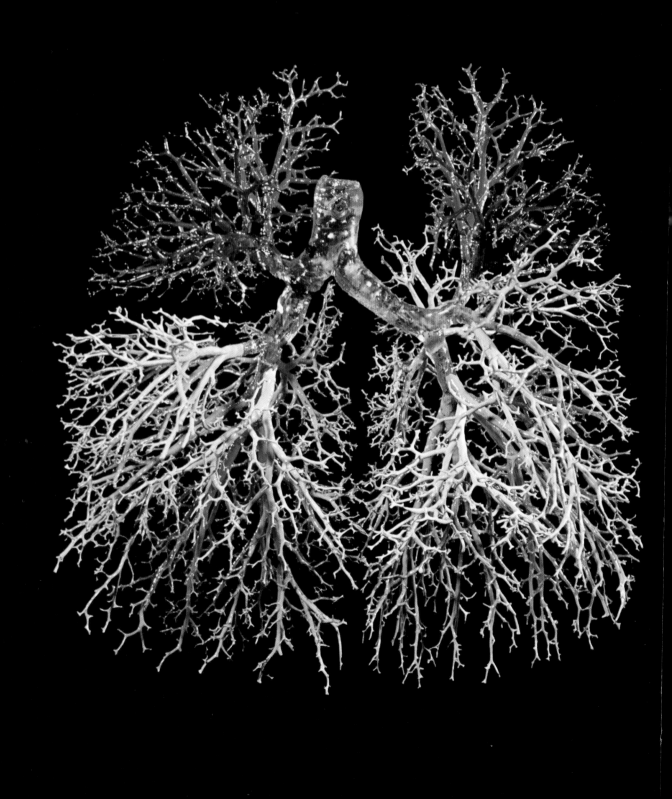

2

Breathe In, Breathe Out

Respiration is involuntary. It is controlled by a part of the brain called the medulla. The medulla signals nerves cells in the diaphragm and tells it when to contract or relax, causing breathing. When people think of breathing, they are usually thinking of inhalation and exhalation. Doctors call the movement of air from the environment into the body through the lungs ventilation. Together, ventilation and the exchange of gases between the lungs and the blood are called external respiration.

A model made of resin shows the different airways that make up the lungs and bronchial tree.

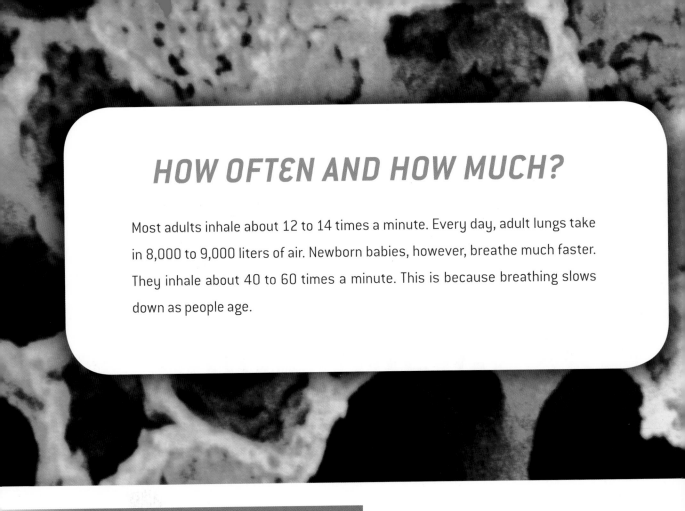

HOW OFTEN AND HOW MUCH?

Most adults inhale about 12 to 14 times a minute. Every day, adult lungs take in 8,000 to 9,000 liters of air. Newborn babies, however, breathe much faster. They inhale about 40 to 60 times a minute. This is because breathing slows down as people age.

OXYGEN AND BLOOD

The body also goes through a process called internal respiration. Internal respiration is the exchange of gases between red blood cells in the circulatory system and the body's tissues. This process starts when oxygen comes into the body through the nose and mouth and ends up in the alveoli of the lungs. Oxygen from inhaled air passes through the walls of the alveoli into the capillaries. Red blood cells flow through the capillaries and special proteins in the blood, called hemoglobin, pick up the oxygen. Each hemoglobin molecule can carry four oxygen molecules. When oxygen binds to the hemoglobin in the red blood cells, the blood becomes oxygenated.

Oxygenated blood flows from the capillaries into larger blood vessels called arteries. Arteries carry the oxygen-rich blood to the heart where it is pumped to other parts of the body. When the oxygenated blood reaches tissue in other parts of the body, the red blood cells once again enter capillaries that surround tissues and organs. The hemoglobin releases the oxygen it is carrying and the gas moves through capillary walls into the surrounding tissue. Here the oxygen can be picked up and used by the body's cells.

Cells release carbon dioxide gas as a waste product. Carbon dioxide and the deoxygenated blood move through blood vessels called veins back

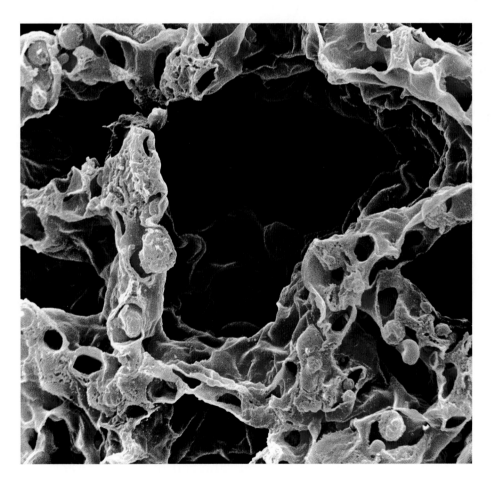

This magnified image shows the alveoli and the walls through which the oxygen and carbon dioxide exchange takes place.

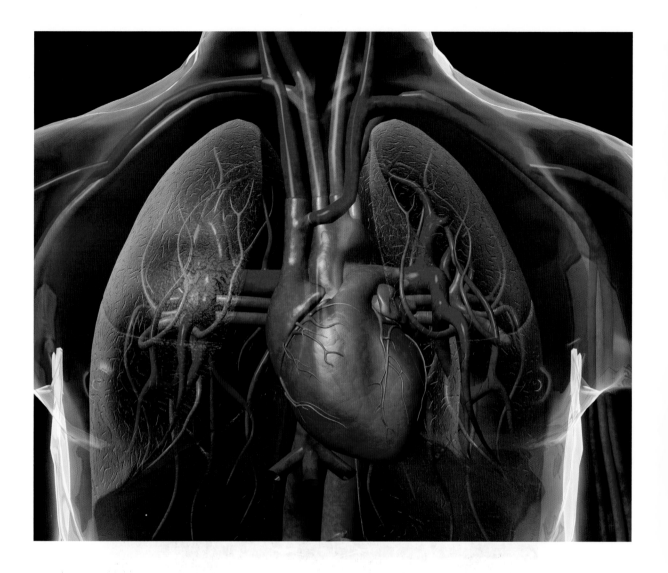

The muscular heart pumps the deoxygenated blood back into the lungs, where the carbon dioxide can then be exhaled.

to the heart. The heart pumps this oxygen-depleted, carbon dioxide-rich blood into the capillaries surrounding the alveoli in the lungs. Carbon dioxide moves through the capillary walls and into the alveoli and is removed from the body by exhalation. The red blood cells pick up more oxygen and the cycle starts over again.

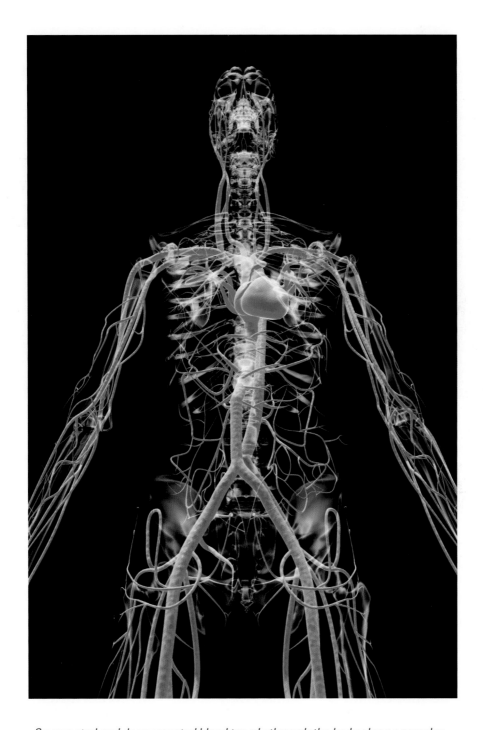

Oxygenated and deoxygenated blood travels through the body along a complex network of blood vessels.

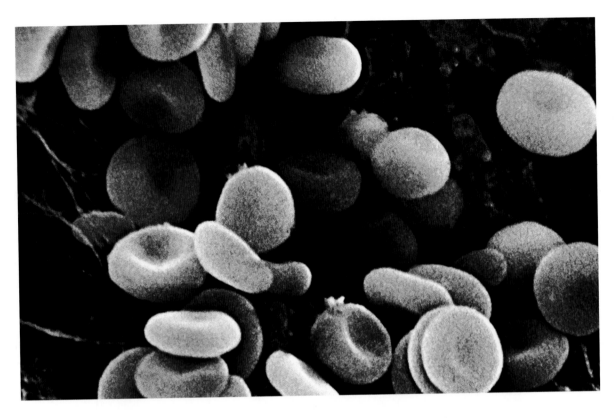

Red blood cells carry oxygen, nutrients, and waste material around the body.

CELLULAR RESPIRATION

Cells use the oxygen delivered by the red blood cells to convert a sugar called glucose into energy. This process is called cellular respiration. Glucose is a simple sugar and is sometimes called blood sugar. The body produces glucose by breaking down carbohydrates in food. For most cells in the body, this simple sugar is the major source of energy.

Inside the cell, cellular respiration takes place in an organelle called the mitochondria. Because they supply the cell with energy, the mitochondria are sometimes called the power plant of the cell. Inside the mitochondria, glucose is combined with oxygen. The chemical reaction between the glucose and the oxygen produces water, carbon dioxide, and energy.

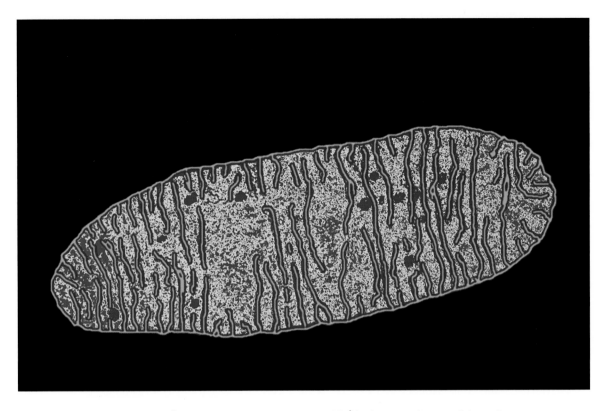

A mitochondrion (the singular form of mitochondria) is the powerhouse of the cell. Depending upon the type and how much energy it needs to produce, a cell might contain hundreds or even thousands of energy-producing mitochondria.

Most of the energy made during cellular respiration is stored. This is similar to the way the energy needed to run a car is stored in a tank of gasoline. In the body, energy is stored within the chemical bonds of a molecule called adenosine triphosphate, or ATP. ATP is used and released when a body needs energy.

AN ACID-BASE BALANCE

Respiration not only supplies the cells with the oxygen they need to carry out cellular respiration, but it also helps the body maintain a healthy acid-base balance. The acid-base balance in the body is very important because the body can only function properly when the blood has just the right pH.

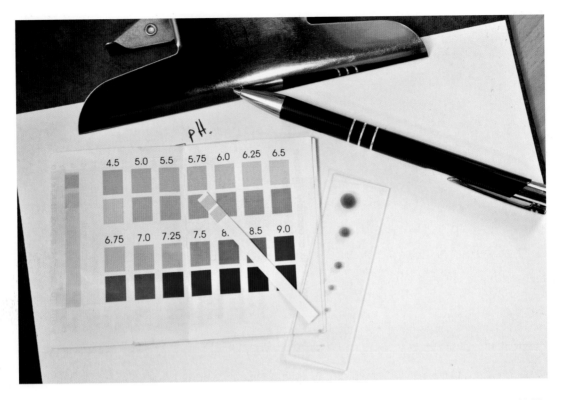

A substance's pH can usually be tested using special test strips that change color based on the pH. The strips are then compared to a color-coded chart that lists the different pH measurements.

The pH of a substance is a measurement of how acidic it is. Lemon juice and vinegar are examples of acids. The pH scale ranges from 0 (very acidic) to 14 (very basic, or alkaline). The pH of both lemon juice and vinegar is around 2. A pH of 7 is neutral. Neutral substances are neither acidic nor basic.

Normal pH for blood is around 7.4. If the pH of the blood falls below 7.35 it is too acidic. If it goes above 7.45 it is too alkaline. Acidic or alkaline blood can severely affect the body's major organs. Therefore, it is very important for the body to control the acid-base balance in the blood. To do this, the brain and the respiratory system work together.

The carbon dioxide that is given off by the body's cells combines with water in the blood. The chemical reaction between carbon dioxide and water forms carbonic acid, a weak acid. If a person's breathing slows down, extra carbon dioxide can build up in the body. This produces more carbonic acid, lowering the pH of the blood and making it more acidic. As blood pH falls, respiratory centers in the brain tell the lungs to increase the rate of respiration. The person breathes faster and releases more carbon dioxide, bringing the body's pH back to normal.

On the other hand, if the pH of the blood becomes too high, the respiratory centers of the brain send a signal to decrease the breathing rate. As the person's breathing slows down, the amount of carbon dioxide in the blood goes up. This, in turn, decreases the pH, and brings the pH of the blood back into balance.

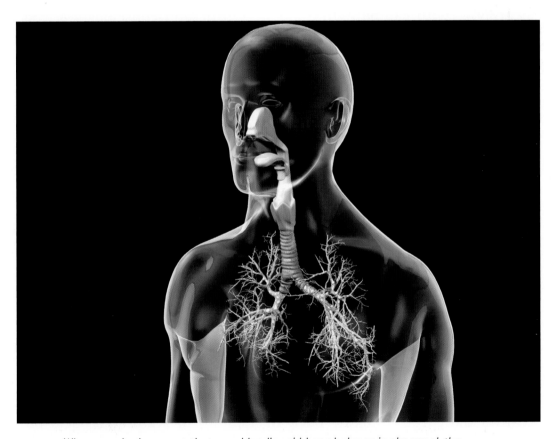

When your body senses that your blood's acid-base balance is abnormal, the brain sends signals that cause the respiratory system to either slow down or speed up. If any of the airways are narrowed or closed up—from disease or damage—this can interfere with maintaining a healthy blood pH, which can lead to serious health problems.

Respiratory Acidosis and Alkalosis

When there is a problem with the body's acid-base balance, respiratory acidosis and alkalosis can occur. In respiratory acidosis, the blood is too acidic. In alkalosis, it is not acidic enough.

Respiratory acidosis is usually a symptom of another, underlying disease. The condition develops when the lungs cannot expel enough carbon dioxide. This may be the result of illnesses such as emphysema, chronic bronchitis, severe pneumonia, or asthma. Symptoms of respiratory acidosis are usually headache and drowsiness. If breathing is severely limited because the lungs are not functioning correctly, this drowsiness can progress within minutes to stupor (a state of semi-consciousness where the person is unaware of their surroundings) or a coma. If breathing is just slightly impaired, the movement from alert to stupor or coma can take several hours. Treatment of respiratory acidosis usually focuses on improving respiratory function. This can be done with medications designed to ease the breathing problem.

Respiratory alkalosis, on the other hand, is caused by rapid, deep breathing, or hyperventilation. Hyperventilation causes too much carbon dioxide to be expelled by the lungs, upsetting the acid-base balance in the body. The most common cause of hyperventilation is anxiety, but it can also be caused by pain, low levels of oxygen in the blood, fever, and aspirin overdose. The symptoms of alkalosis can range from no symptoms at all, to muscle twitching and cramping, and progress to severe muscle spasms. Slowing the breathing is usually the only treatment needed for respiratory alkalosis. Breathing into a paper bag (not a plastic one) may also help. The bag captures the carbon dioxide being exhaled. The person breathes the carbon dioxide back in, helping to restore the acid-base balance and relieving the symptoms of alkalosis.

WHY DO WE YAWN?

Many people believe that we yawn because we are tired or bored. It is true that people yawn more during these times, but most scientists agree that yawning serves some other purpose. They just do not know what that purpose might be. The most common scientific theory is that yawning is an involuntary, respiratory reflex used to supply our lungs with more oxygen. Scientists think that it is possible that we yawn more when we are tired or bored because we breathe more slowly during these times, making our bodies need more oxygen.

However, this theory does not explain why people yawn when they see someone else yawn. Or why babies—who are still in their mother's womb and do not even breath oxygen yet—have been seen yawning during ultrasound exams!

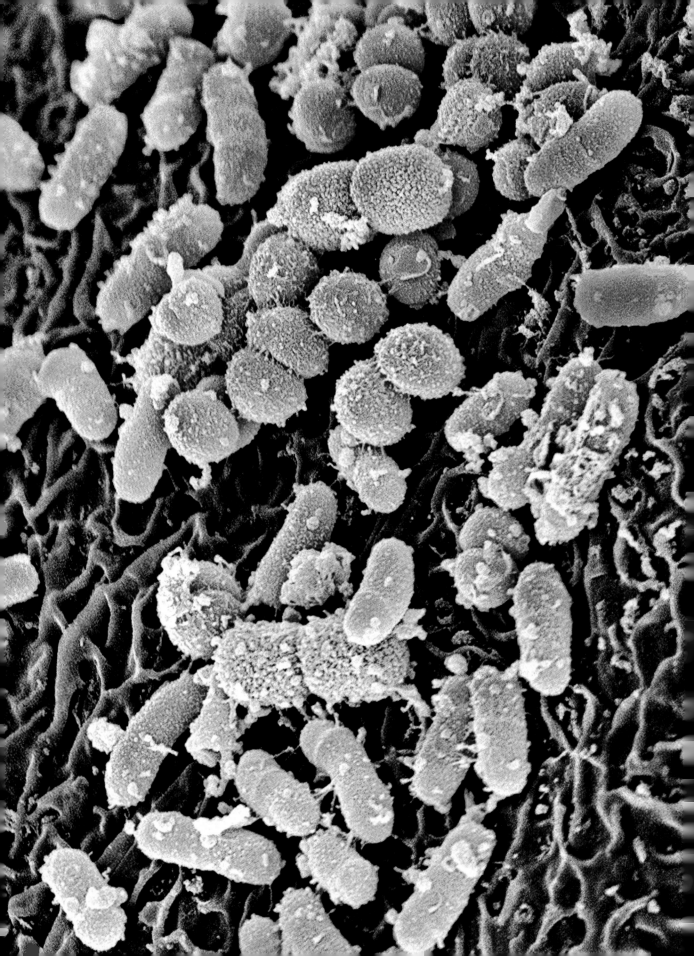

3

Breathless

Many different things can affect breathing. Respiratory organs that are damaged or improperly developed can cause respiratory problems. However, illnesses or diseases are the most common causes of breathing problems.

INFECTIONS

Because the upper respiratory tract includes the sinuses, nasal passages, pharynx, and larynx, infections such as the common cold, flu, sinus infections, tonsillitis (inflamed tonsils), and laryngitis (inflammation

Bacteria (orange) can cause infections of the respiratory system.

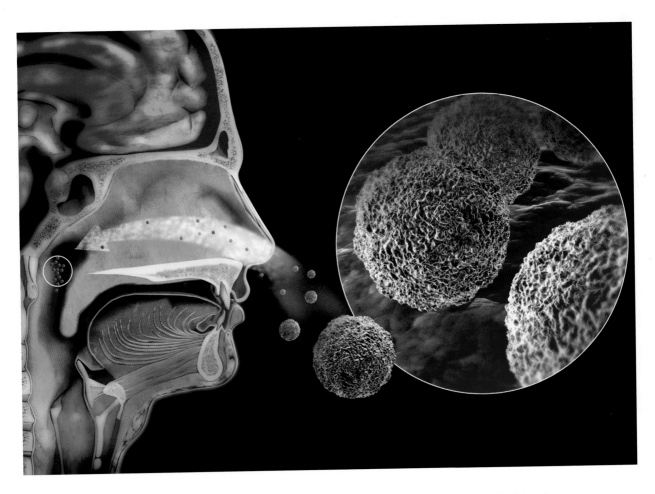

A person can be infected by viruses, such as the ones that cause the common cold, if the virus particles are in the air.

of the larynx) are all considered upper respiratory tract infections (URIs). Occasionally, a URI is caused by a bacterial infection, but most URIs are caused by viruses. In fact, there are more than two hundred different viruses that cause URIs.

The viruses that cause URIs are spread by coughing, sneezing, or personal contact with someone infected by one of the viruses, for example by hugging them or shaking hands with them. The viruses can also be passed by touching something an infected person has touched, such as a doorknob or tissue, and then touching mucous membranes in your nose, mouth, or eyes.

WHY DOES THE COLD VIRUS LIKE COLD WEATHER?

People can be infected with the common cold virus at anytime of the year, but most Americans "catch" colds in the fall and winter. Scientists believe the higher number of infections during the colder months may be caused by people remaining indoors. This puts people in closer contact for longer periods of time during the winter.

While this may be true, researchers at the National Institute of Health (NIH) may have found another reason that has to do more with the virus itself. In March 2008, the NIH scientists discovered that the outer coating of the influenza virus (the virus that causes the flu) toughens up in cooler temperatures. They believe that this stronger outer coating, called the envelope, helps the virus survive longer outside the human body. If the virus can live longer outside a human host, it can linger around long enough to infect another person. Scientists are not sure yet if the envelope on the virus that causes the common cold also gets stronger in colder weather, but they think this may explain why people catch more colds in the wintertime.

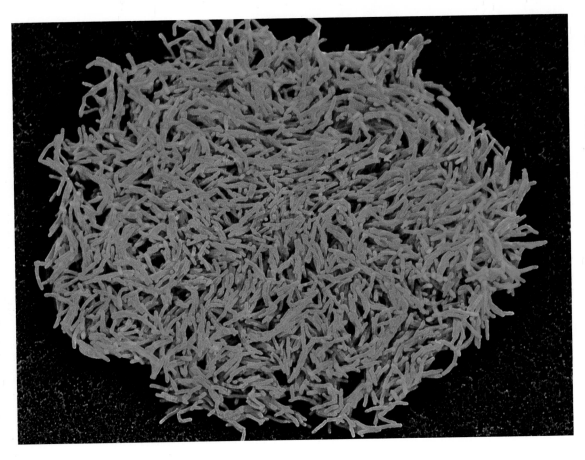

This microscopic image shows the bacteria that can cause tuberculosis.

TUBERCULOSIS

Colds and flu are not the only respiratory illness passed from person to person. Tuberculosis (TB), another contagious disease, is not caused by a virus, but by bacteria that attacks the lungs. Like the cold or flu virus, the bacteria that cause TB can be spread through the air. This usually happens when someone with an active case of TB coughs or sneezes. Bacteria trapped in droplets expelled from the TB patient's nose or mouth can be inhaled by people in the surrounding area, infecting them.

Symptoms of active TB disease include chest pain and a long-lasting cough that is often accompanied by bloody phlegm. Not everyone who inhales the bacteria that causes TB develops an active case of the disease, however. In most people, their immune system detects and destroys the TB bacteria before it starts growing. However, the bacteria may still be alive in these people's bodies. This is called a latent TB infection. Latent means that the bacteria are present in the body, but the patient has no symptoms. Because there are no symptoms, a person with a latent TB infection does not feel sick. They also cannot spread the disease. Many people with a latent TB infection live their entire lives not knowing that the bacteria are present in their bodies. However, it is possible for the latent bacteria to become active. The bacteria in a person with active TB disease is living, dividing, and spreading throughout the person's body. If it is not treated, the bacteria can spread beyond the lungs to other vital organs such as the kidneys, spine, and brain.

At one time, TB was the leading cause of death in the United States. But in the 1940s, doctors discovered antibiotics (medications that can destroy or slow the growth of bacteria) that could kill the TB bacteria. These medications helped to control the spread of

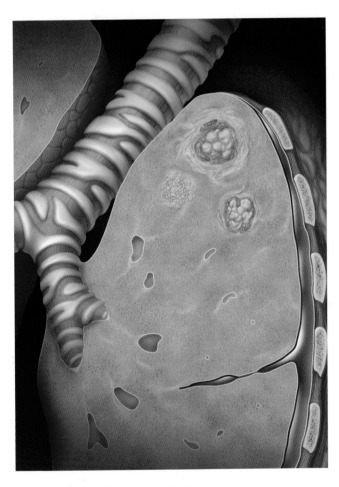

Untreated or serious cases of tuberculosis can cause lesions, or damaged areas, in the lungs.

the disease and the number of TB cases declined—until 1985. Between 1985 and 1992, the number of cases of TB increased. This increase was a result of budget cuts to programs that were designed to control TB, the first appearance of the virus that causes acquired immune deficiency syndrome (AIDS) in America, and drug-resistant strains of TB that were not killed by regular antibiotics. By the early 1990s, however, the number of active TB cases started to decrease. This was due to increased funding to TB control programs and the discovery of ways to prevent the spread of the virus that causes AIDS. Fortunately, the number of active TB cases has been dropping ever since.

However, TB is still a problem in the United States today. The bacteria that cause TB die very slowly. In fact, it can take as long as six months to kill all of the TB bacteria in the body. Once treatment is started, however, TB patients often start to feel better in just a couple of weeks. Because their symptoms have disappeared, some patients believe that it is safe to stop taking the antibiotics prescribed to control their disease. But it is not. When a patient stops taking antibiotics too early, not all of the bacteria are killed. This can cause the patient to relapse (all of their symptoms come back) and it can leave behind drug-resistant bacteria that can be much harder to treat.

SARS

Like the common cold and the flu, TB has been around for a very long time. But sometimes new strains of bacteria or viruses that have never been seen before in humans can develop. This is what happened with a new disease called severe acute respiratory syndrome (SARS) that first emerged in China in 2002. SARS is caused by a new strain of the same kind of virus that causes the common cold.

During the 2003 SARS outbreak, travelers quickly spread the disease to North America, South America, and Europe. By the time the outbreak subsided, 8,000 people had been infected with the virus. About 10 percent (800 people) died of the disease. SARS was the first serious, contagious disease to develop in the twenty-first century. At this time, doctors do not have an effective treatment for SARS.

PNEUMONIA

One complication that can result from a respiratory illness such as SARS or the flu is an inflammation, or swelling, of the lungs. Inflammation of the lungs is called pneumonia. About half of pneumonia cases are caused by viruses. But viruses are not the only infectious microorganisms that cause pneumonia, bacterial or fungal infections can also cause pneumonia.

Most of the time, the inflammation occurs in only one lung. If both lungs are involved, the condition is called double pneumonia. A patient with pneumonia generally has symptoms such as coughing, chest pain, fever, chills, and shortness of breath.

Healthy cilia in the respiratory tract usually prevent germs and foreign material from entering the alveoli, but sometimes things get through and cause infections and illness.

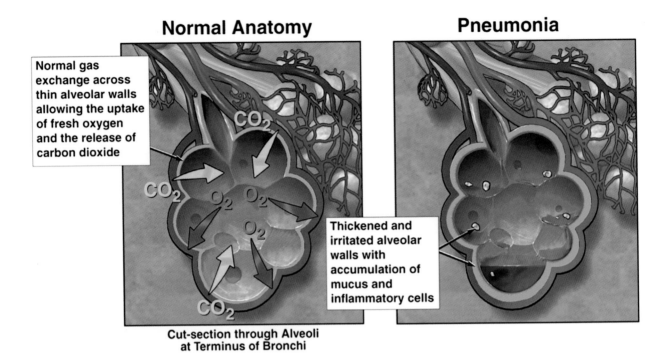

Normal Anatomy

Normal gas exchange across thin alveolar walls allowing the uptake of fresh oxygen and the release of carbon dioxide

CO_2

CO_2

O_2 O_2

O_2

CO_2

Cut-section through Alveoli at Terminus of Bronchi

Pneumonia

Thickened and irritated alveolar walls with accumulation of mucus and inflammatory cells

For a person suffering from pneumonia, the buildup of mucus and fluids in the alveoli (right) affects the normal exchange of oxygen and carbon dioxide (left).

Bacterial pneumonia also produces a lot of thick, greenish or yellow phlegm. Viral pneumonia patients, on the other hand, cough up very small amounts of clear or white phlegm.

Bacterial pneumonia can be treated with antibiotics, but, like TB, antibiotic-resistant strains of pneumonia-causing bacteria are a growing problem. Antibiotics do not work on viral pneumonia. There are a few antiviral medications that doctors may prescribe, but many times, the only treatment for viral pneumonia is the same as that for the flu—a lot of rest and plenty of fluids.

Along with viruses and bacteria, pneumonia can also be caused by a microscopic organism called mycoplasma. The symptoms of pneumonia caused by mycoplasma are usually milder than pneumonia caused by bacteria or viruses. Because the symptoms are often not bad enough to send people to the doctor or hospital, this type of pneumonia is sometimes called "walking pneumonia."

People come into contact with the bacteria, viruses, and other organisms that can cause pneumonia every day. Normally, the microscopic hairs that line the airways sweep these microorganisms up and out of the lungs. But even when some of these microorganisms get past the cilia and into the lungs they rarely cause pneumonia because the body's immune system detects and kills them. Occasionally, however, they are able to overwhelm the immune system and pneumonia develops. The elderly and people with chronic health problems, especially those with reoccurring respiratory illnesses, are more likely to develop pneumonia than people with healthy, functioning immune systems.

ASTHMA

The inflammation that causes pneumonia is a short-term respiratory illness. But about 20 million Americans (almost 9 million of whom are children) suffer from chronic, or long-term, inflammation of the airways. People who have chronically inflamed airways have asthma.

The inflammation causes the airways in a person with asthma to become very sensitive and causes them

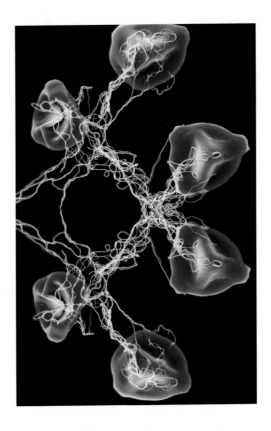

Microscopic debris, like pollen from plants and trees, can inflame the airways and interfere with respiration in a person with asthma.

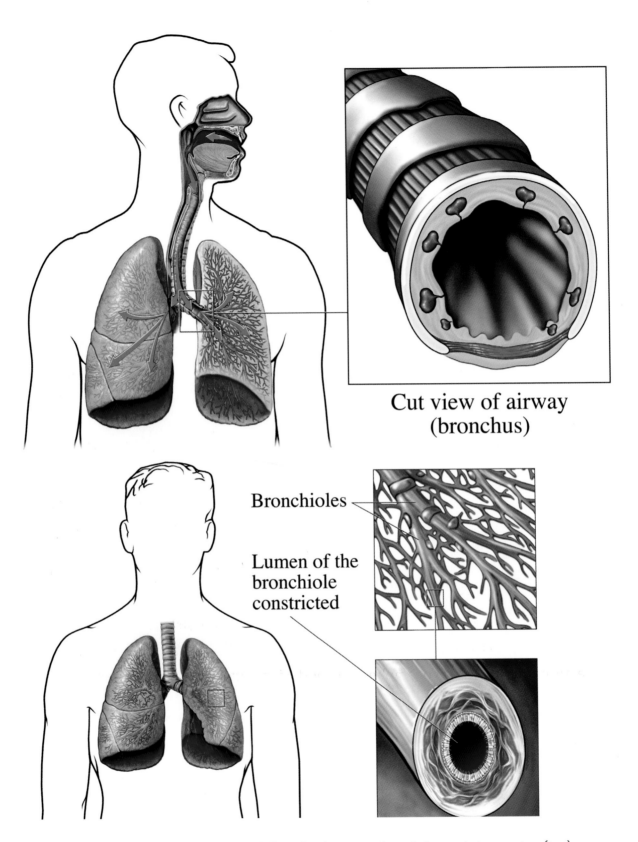

Cut view of airway
(bronchus)

Bronchioles

Lumen of the
bronchiole
constricted

Normally, the airway is open wide and allows for air to move through the respiratory system (top).
During an asthma attack, the bronchioles constrict, or narrow, blocking airflow (bottom).

to react strongly to irritants such as dust, pollen, and smoke. If an asthma sufferer comes into contact with something that they are allergic to, this can cause the inflammation to get worse. When this happens, muscles surrounding the airways contract and squeeze making the airways smaller. Irritated airways also produce more mucus than non-irritated ones. The build-up of mucus narrows the breathing passages even more. The narrower airways make it hard to breathe and the person suffers an asthma attack. During an asthma attack, the person might cough or wheeze (make a high-pitched whistling noise in the chest when breathing).

Doctors cannot cure asthma, but the disease can be controlled by medication. Most asthma medications are inhaled. Because they are inhaled, the drugs go straight to the lungs where they are needed the most and can work quickly to reduce the inflammation. To prevent asthma attacks, people who have asthma should see their doctors regularly to make sure that their asthma stays under control. Most asthma sufferers also learn which irritants trigger their asthma attacks and try to stay away from those things as much as possible. Triggers are different in different people. Some people may be allergic to pet dander (dead skin cells) and being around dogs or cats can trigger an asthma attack in those people. Cold air can trigger other people's asthma. These asthma sufferers have to be careful to cover their mouth and nose with a scarf when they venture outdoors on very cold days. Other triggers may include dust, pollen, mold, certain foods, tobacco smoke, air pollution, exercise, and respiratory infections (such as a cold or flu).

Some asthma attacks can be worse than others. A severe asthma attack can almost completely close the airways. This can prevent oxygen from reaching vital organs such as the heart and brain. Because oxygen deprivation to the heart and brain can cause death, severe asthma attacks should be treated as a medical emergency and victims should be taken to the closest hospital emergency room.

Doctors are not exactly sure what causes some people to develop asthma while others do not. However, they do know that the condition often runs in families. Children related to someone with asthma are more likely to develop the disease than a child with no family history of asthma. The disease is also closely associated with allergies. While not all people who have asthma also have allergies, most do. Some scientific studies have shown that exposure to tobacco smoke, certain infections at an early age, and some

Most people with asthma use an inhaler to ease the symptoms. The inhaler delivers special medication that widens the constricted airways.

allergens (such as animal dander, mold, or pollen) may also increase a person's risk of developing asthma.

Most people with asthma develop the condition in childhood. But anyone of any age can be diagnosed with asthma. In childhood, more boys than girls are diagnosed with asthma, but in adulthood, more women than men have the disease.

CYSTIC FIBROSIS

Cystic Fibrosis (CF) is caused by a mutation, or an abnormal change in a person's genetic material. A person's genetic material is responsible

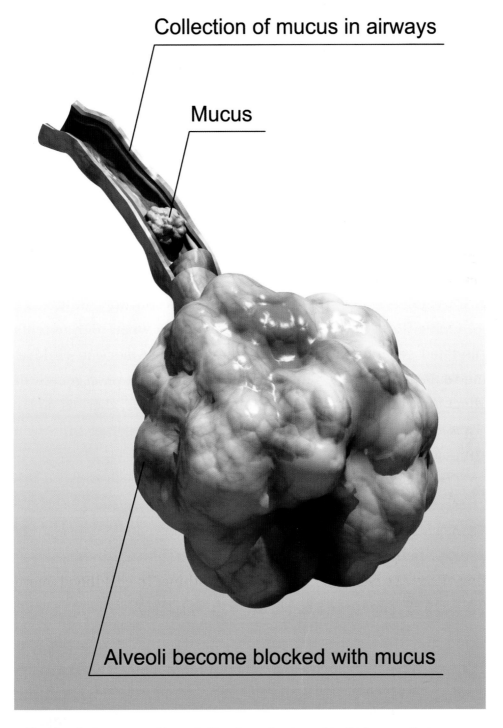

Collection of mucus in airways

Mucus

Alveoli become blocked with mucus

The alveoli of a person with cystic fibrosis can be clogged by thick mucus that impedes respiration.

for determining physical characteristics and how the body grows and functions. Mutations in genetic material cause the cells in the body to not function properly. Mutations can occur as a result of exposure to dangerous chemicals, but mutations can also occur for no known reason. Some genetic mutations are passed from parent to child.

The mutation in a CF patient's cells causes their mucus to be abnormally thick and sticky. The mucus blocks the airways in the lungs and makes it difficult to breathe. The sticky mucus also traps bacteria that can cause serious, recurring lung infections. After many repeated infections, a CF patient's lung tissue can become permanently scarred. This scarring can result in respiratory failure in which the lungs stop working. Most CF patients eventually die as a result of respiratory failure.

Cystic fibrosis is usually passed to a child when both parents have the mutated genetic material. More than 30,000 American children and young adults live with CF. This makes CF the most common genetic disease to affect the lungs in the United States. At this time, there is no cure for CF. However, therapies and medication that help loosen or thin the mucus help many people with CF.

Treatments continue to improve and researchers are looking for ways to cure or prevent CF. This is great progress because before the 1980s, most CF patients died in childhood or early adolescence. Today, the average lifespan for a patient with CF is more than 35 years.

PHYSICAL PROBLEMS

Diseases and illness are not the only things that can make a person breathless. When food or some other foreign object blocks the upper airway, a person chokes. Because the object blocks the flow of air into the lungs, a person who is choking will have difficulty breathing, be unable to speak, and cannot cough forcefully enough to dislodge the object from

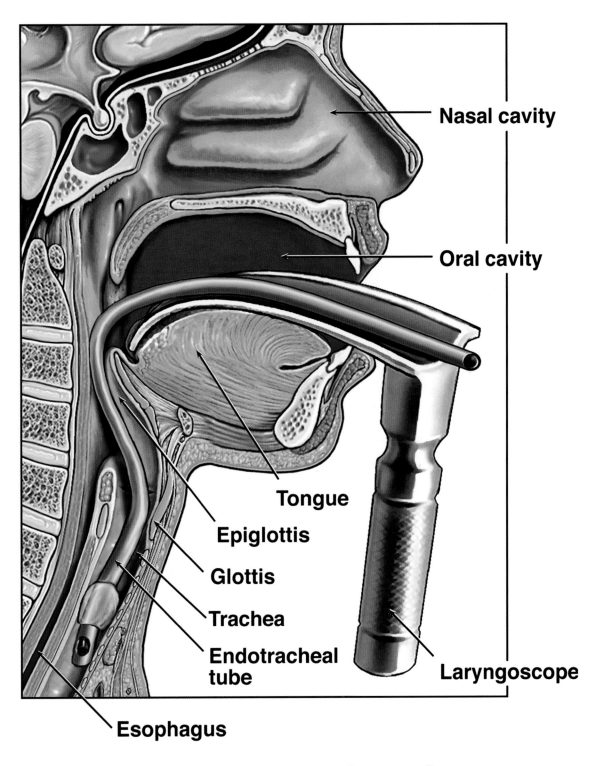

Nasal cavity

Oral cavity

Tongue

Epiglottis

Glottis

Trachea

Endotracheal tube

Laryngoscope

Esophagus

Sometimes, if an airway is blocked a doctor must use a laryngoscope. The laryngoscope is inserted into the mouth and a tube that will aid respiration is guided down the trachea.

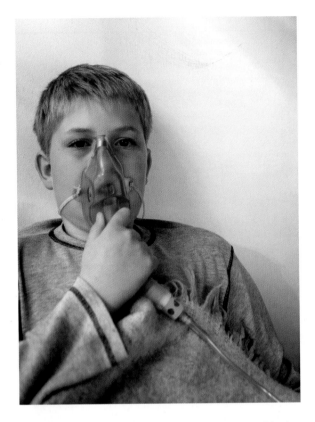

People who have trouble breathing because of faulty gas exchange in the lungs are sometimes given oxygen to help make breathing easier.

their airway. The Heimlich maneuver is usually performed on people who are choking. It involves pushing against the diaphragm to force the object out.

Collapsed Lung

A collapsed lung occurs when air builds up in the pleural space, between the chest wall and the lung. The build up of air causes pressure. The pressure presses on the lung and causes it to collapse. A collapsed lung is most often caused by an injury to the chest wall or a hole in the lung. For example, a broken rib can puncture a lung and cause air to escape into the pleural space. To release the pressure, the air in the pleural space must be removed to allow the lung to reinflate. Sometimes this occurs naturally.

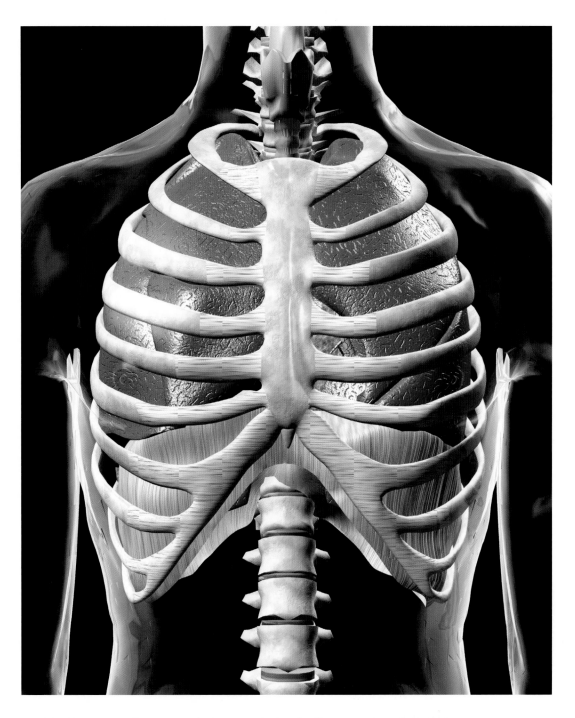

The ribcage usually protects the lungs and other fragile organs, but a broken rib can puncture a lung and lead to breathing problems.

If it does not, a doctor may remove the air with a needle and syringe. The doctor may also use a hollow plastic tube called a chest tube that is attached to a device that can suck the air out of the chest.

SLEEP APNEA AND SNORING

Breathing is involuntary and controlled by the brain without your having to think about it. But in some people, these brain signals malfunction during the night. This causes a condition called sleep apnea. People who suffer from sleep apnea can stop breathing more than three hundred times a night for as long as ten seconds at a time. Sleep apnea can also be caused by

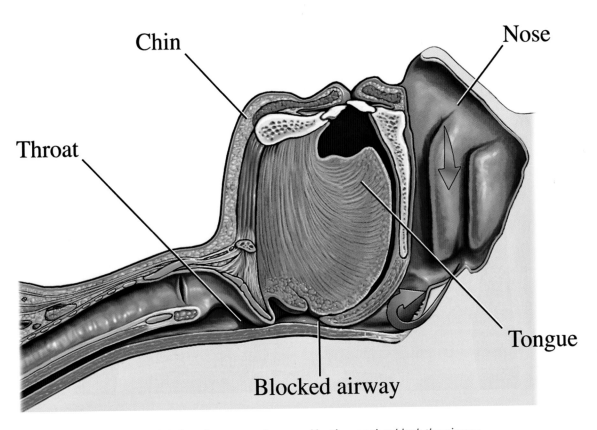

Many experts think that sleep apnea is caused by tissues that block the airway during sleep.

things that block the airways, such as swollen or deformed tonsils or tissues.

Most people do not realize that they have sleep apnea, but family members may notice the loud snoring, snorting, or choking sounds that often accompany the condition. Sleep apnea is a very serious condition and it is a good idea for people who suspect they have sleep apnea to be checked by a doctor. The doctor can make sure the person is breathing correctly when he or she sleeps. Medication, surgery, and special breathing machines can sometimes help people with sleep apnea.

Snoring is often a symptom of sleep apnea, but not all people who snore have sleep apnea. Snoring is caused when air movement through the airways is somehow obstructed or blocked. This can result from a stuffy nose, swollen airways, weak muscles in the throat, or problems with the uvula and palate. People who are overweight and older people are most likely to snore. Snoring is not usually a serious problem for most people, but if it interferes with sleeping or breathing properly it is best to talk to a doctor about it.

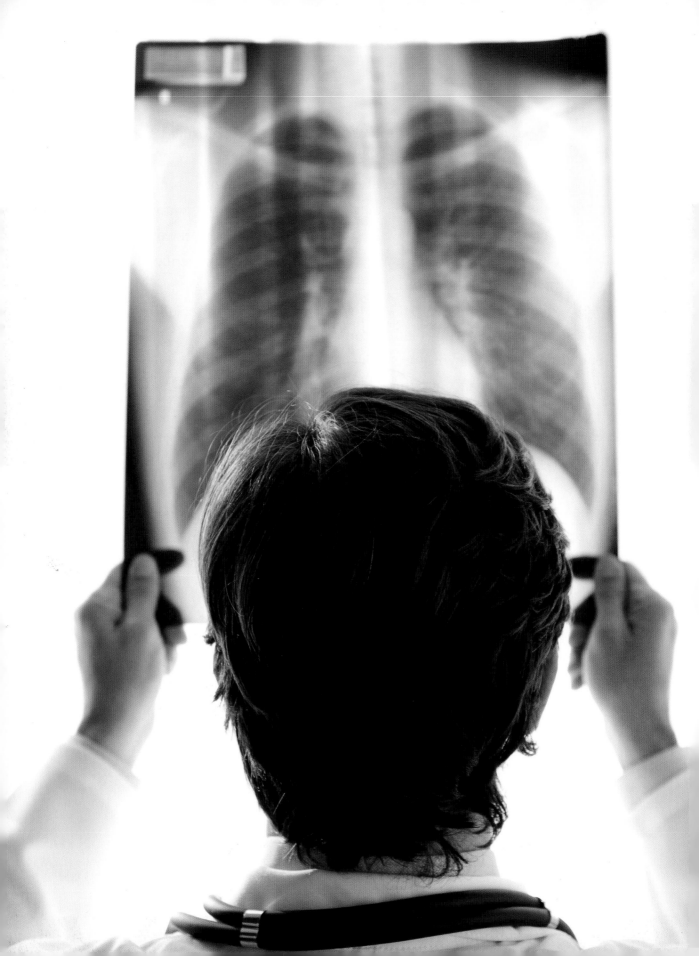

4

Healthy Lungs

Assuming they do not have a respiratory illness or disease, young adults usually have the highest lung capacity. This means that their lungs can take in large amounts of air. At this age, the lungs are also at their healthiest. As people grow older, lung volume and lung health naturally start to decline. However, keeping in good physical shape, staying away from things that can damage your lungs, and making smart lifestyle choices can have a positive effect on the health of your lungs.

X rays can often help doctors determine if lungs and airways are healthy and unblocked.

SMOKING

The lifestyle choice that has the largest effect on a person's lungs is whether or not the person decides to smoke. Whether a person smokes cigarettes, cigars, or a pipe they inhale tobacco smoke directly into their lungs. This is especially harmful because tobacco smoke contains more than 4,000 toxic, or poisonous, chemicals. Scientists have determined that at least 40 of these chemicals are carcinogens. Carcinogens are chemicals that are known to cause cancer.

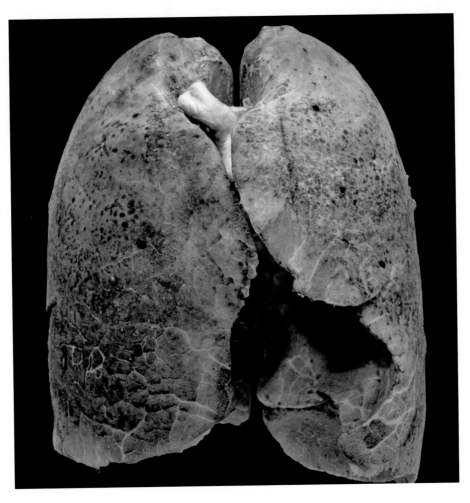

Healthy lungs should be pink and red. The dark unhealthy lungs shown here were taken from a smoker who died from lung problems.

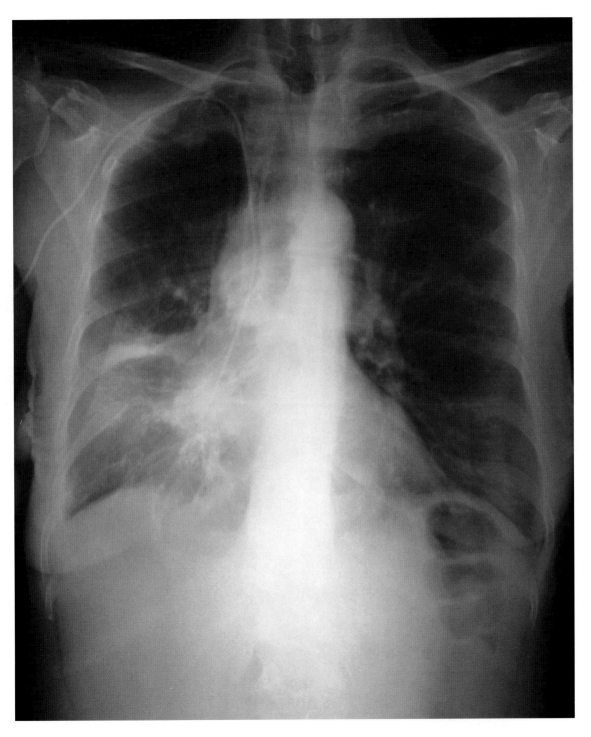

The orange and yellow masses in this X ray are cancerous tumors caused by smoking.

Carcinogens cause cancer by damaging the genetic material that controls cell growth and development. When this material gets damaged, cells can grow out of control and cause cancer. Inhaling tobacco smoke delivers the carcinogens in the smoke directly to the lungs. From the lungs, the carcinogens can move through the walls of the alveoli directly into the capillaries surrounding them. This allows the toxic chemicals to be distributed throughout the rest of the body by the bloodstream. This is why smoking also increases the risk of developing cancer of the nose, mouth, salivary glands, vocal cords, esophagus, bladder, pancreas, and kidneys.

Unfortunately, people can develop lung cancer from the secondhand smoke of others.

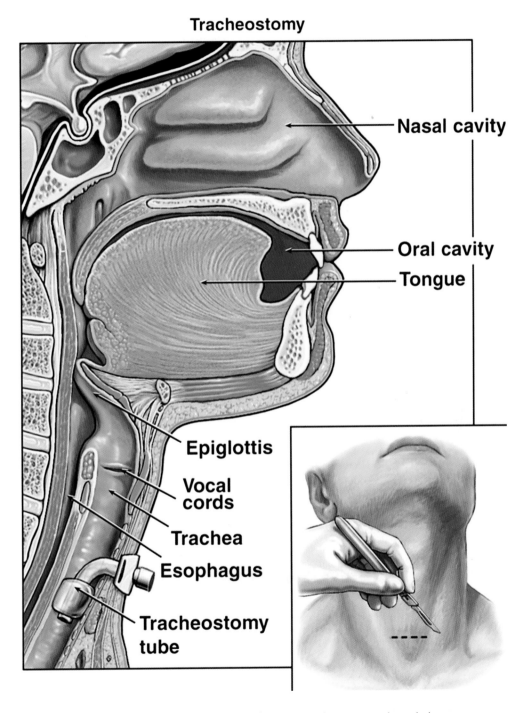

Tracheostomy

Nasal cavity

Oral cavity

Tongue

Epiglottis

Vocal cords

Trachea

Esophagus

Tracheostomy tube

When breathing becomes difficult, doctors may insert a tracheostomy tube to help a person breathe. People who have damaged their airways with long-term smoking may need these tubes.

Smokers are five to ten times more likely to develop lung cancer than non-smokers. In fact, about 87 percent of lung cancer deaths are caused by smoking. About 160,000 Americans die of lung cancer every year. More than 140,000 of these people are or were smokers at some time during their lifetime. Lung cancer is the leading cause of cancer death for both men and women in the United States.

Smoking also accounts for 82 percent of voice box cancers, 80 to 90 percent of cancers of the esophagus, 40 percent of bladder cancers, 30 percent of pancreatic cancers, and 17 percent of kidney cancer cases. Women who smoke also have an increased risk of developing cervical cancer (a part of the reproductive system) and men have a higher risk of developing cancer of the penis. Together, cancers caused by smoking account for about one-third of all cancer deaths and smokers are twice as likely to die of cancer as nonsmokers. The risk is even higher in heavy smokers.

Secondhand Smoke

Even if a person does not smoke, he or she can still be harmed by tobacco smoke. Non-smokers inhale secondhand smoke when they are near people who are smoking. A non-smoker is 20 to 30 percent more likely to develop lung cancer when exposed to secondhand smoke at home or at work. Babies and children who are exposed to secondhand smoke are much more likely to develop lower respiratory infections than children who are not exposed to smoke. Scientists have also linked sudden infant death syndrome (SIDS) to the inhalation of secondhand smoke.

People who have impaired lung function to begin with-for example, people with asthma or emphysema-are especially susceptible to lung irritation due to tobacco smoke. Smoking or inhaling secondhand smoke can also aggravate asthma symptoms and bring on a severe asthma attack in many asthmatics.

COPD

Chronic Obstructive Pulmonary Disease (COPD) describes both emphysema and chronic bronchitis. Emphysema is a disease in which the alveoli in the lungs are damaged. The walls of healthy alveoli contain elastic fibers that allow the tiny air sacs to expand, like a balloon, when you inhale. Inhaled toxins can damage these elastic fibers and they lose their stretchiness. This can cause the air sacs to overstretch and rupture. When alveoli are overstretched or have ruptured, it makes it harder to expel air in the lungs.

Toxic chemicals can also paralyze the tiny hair-like cilia in the lungs. The cilia normally sweep mucus containing inhaled debris up and out of the lungs. When the cilia are paralyzed, the toxins can sit in the lungs longer. The longer these toxins are in contact with the walls of the alveoli, the more damage they can do. Emphysema develops over a long period of time. By the time most people suffer from symptoms of the disease irreparable damage to the lungs has already been done. There is no cure for this disease, though some medications and surgery may help a person with emphysema breathe more easily.

Most cases of emphysema are caused by smoking. However, breathing in secondhand smoke also increases a person's risk of developing emphysema. The best way to prevent emphysema is to not smoke and reduce your exposure to secondhand smoke.

Chronic Bronchitis

Smokers are also more likely to develop chronic bronchitis. Bronchitis occurs when the lining of the bronchial tubes becomes irritated and produces excess mucus. This causes a chronic (long-term) cough as the person tries to cough mucus up and out of their lungs. Because mucus stays longer in the respiratory system, it can become infected. If the mucus is

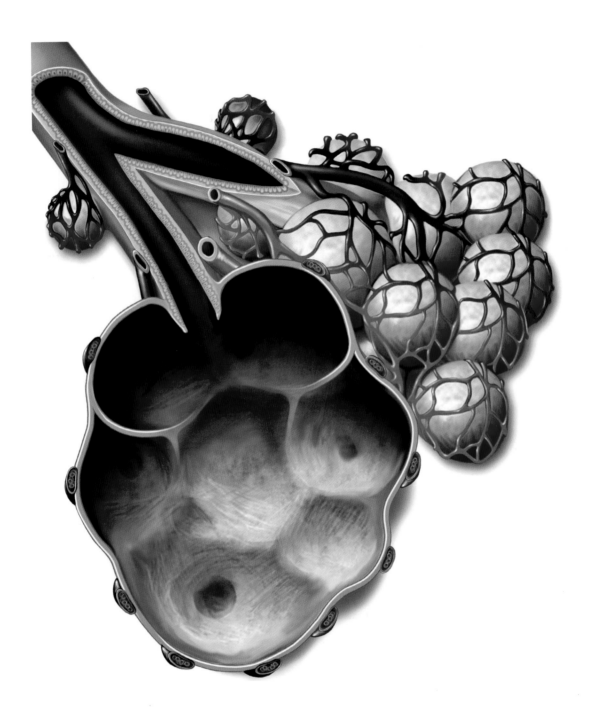

Emphysema has destroyed the walls of these alveoli. Without healthy alveolar wall, the gas exchange needed for respiration is affected.

infected, it often takes on a yellowish-gray or green color. Normal mucus is clear. People with chronic bronchitis usually have permanent lung damage.

Anyone, nonsmokers and smokers alike, can suffer from the occasional bout of acute bronchitis. Acute bronchitis is often caused by a respiratory infection, such as a cold or flu virus. The difference between chronic bronchitis and acute bronchitis is that

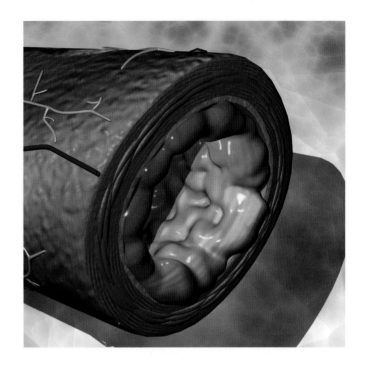

Bronchitis occurs when the bronchial tubes become inflamed and blocked by mucus.

acute bronchitis usually clears up in a day or two, though the cough can last longer. Chronic bronchitis, on the other hand, can persist for several months at a time and it tends to reoccur frequently. Also, unlike chronic bronchitis, acute bronchitis rarely results in permanent lung damage.

CHOOSING NOT TO SMOKE

Because smoking can damage the cilia, alveoli, and bronchioles in the lungs, it can impair lung function. Between the damage it does to the lungs and the increase in risk of developing cancer, smoking is, all around, a very bad idea for the body. But it is much easier to decide to never start

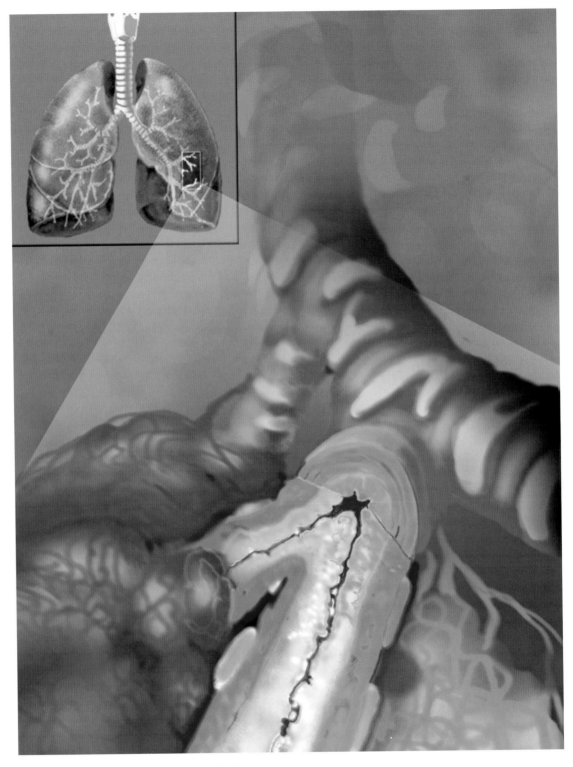

Chronic bronchitis can permanently damage the airways.

smoking than it is to stop smoking. This is because nicotine, one of the chemicals in tobacco, is an addictive drug. That means that once you start using a lot of it, your body feels like it will always need it. Stopping tobacco use may be difficult, but it is necessary for a long and healthy life. Many of the health problems that face smokers can be greatly reduced and, sometimes, even reversed by kicking the habit.

PREVENTING INFECTIONS

Every year a lot of people are forced into bed by the viruses that cause the common cold and the flu. Once you have been infected, there is nothing to do except get plenty of rest and drink a lot of fluids. However, there are some things that you can try that might help you avoid getting infected to begin with.

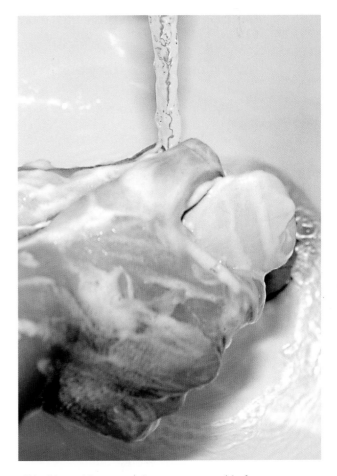

You are more likely to develop an upper respiratory infection if you are under physical or mental stress. Not getting enough sleep, not eating a healthy diet, and smoking can put your body under physical stress. So avoiding stressful situations, getting plenty of sleep, eating well, and not smoking can help your body's defense system ward off those viruses. Washing your hands often can help,

Washing with soap and water can get rid of many germs on your hands. If your hands are dirty, remember not to touch your mouth, nose, or face since respiratory infections can be spread that way.

too. Bacteria and viruses can enter your body when you eat or touch your face, nose, eyes, or mouth, with dirty hands.

Once you have a cold or the flu, you can also help prevent spreading the viruses to others. Whenever you sneeze of cough, turn away from others and use a tissue to cover your mouth and nose. Throw away the tissue after using it and be sure to washing your hands after sneezing, coughing, or blowing your nose.

EXERCISE

Getting plenty of physical exercise can help keep the lungs healthy. During exercise, muscle cells need more oxygen to burn. Because they burn more oxygen, they also release more carbon dioxide. When the brain

Exercising can help keep your weight down, but also strengthens your muscles, your heart, and can help improve your breathing.

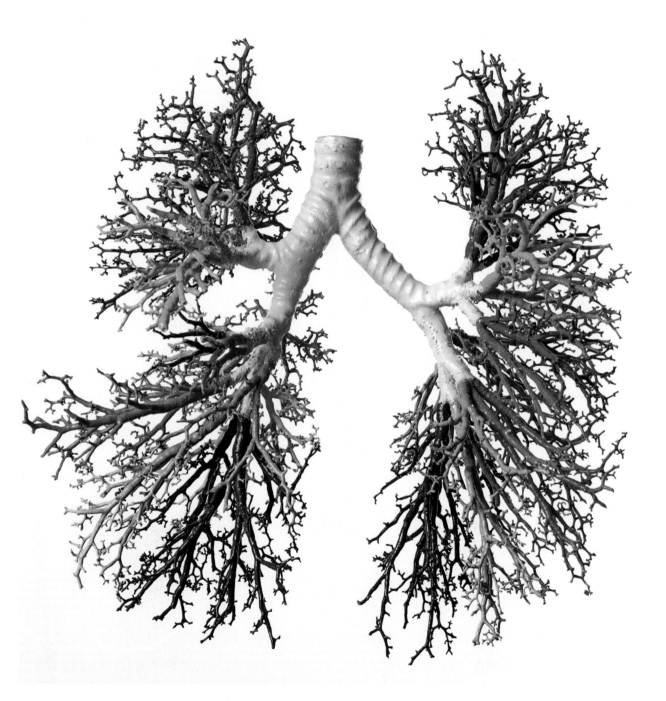

Exercising increases blood flow to your heart and the rest of your body, which also makes your lungs work harder.

detects a rise in carbon dioxide levels, it signals the lungs to increase the respiratory rate (speed) and volume. This increase in rate and volume increases the amount of oxygen taken in and the amount of carbon dioxide expelled. The heart rate also goes up so that the circulatory system can pick up oxygenated blood and deliver it to the muscles more quickly. This increased pumping of blood also transports carbon dioxide away from the muscle cells and back to the lungs where it can be exhaled.

Unlike muscles, the lungs do not get bigger or stronger with increased physical activity. However, regular long-term exercise does strengthen the respiratory system in general. The diaphragm and the intercostals, for example, are muscles. Because they are muscles they do get stronger with regular exercise. A stronger diaphragm and intercostals can make the chest cavity bigger. A larger chest cavity allows for a larger lung capacity.

With regular exercise, more capillaries form around the alveoli, too. This means that more gas exchange can take place. So even though the lungs do not get any bigger, regular exercise makes the respiratory system stronger by allowing the lungs to work more efficiently.

Regular exercise can also help you maintain a healthy weight. Some breathing problems are caused by being overweight and unhealthy. By controlling your weight you can prevent some respiratory issues and also improve you all-around health.

VISIT YOUR DOCTOR

Regular exams with your doctor are necessary for your overall health. A doctor can keep track of how you are growing and if you are developing any health issues. If you feel like you are having some breathing problems or if you have a cold that is not getting better, you should go to your

To diagnose, or determine, breathing problems, doctors often use an instrument called a spirometer. When a patient breathes into a mouthpiece attached to the spirometer, the instrument measures the air flow into and out of the lungs. It also measures how much air the lungs can hold.

Doctors may also want to measure how much gas is exchanged through the alveoli and capillary membranes. To do this, a harmless gas is put into the spirometer. The patient breathes in the gas and the difference in the amount of gas inhaled and

the amount of gas that is exhaled can be calculated. The difference in these amounts can tell the physician how quickly gas can travel from the lungs into the bloodstream. These kinds of tests are called pulmonary function tests, or PFTs.

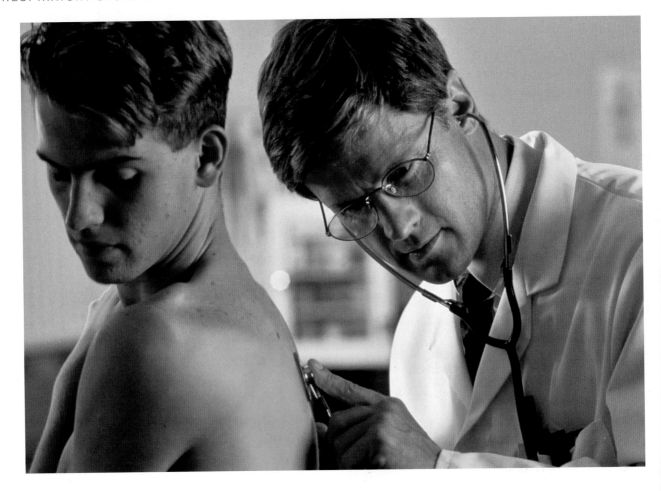

During a regular health checkup, your doctor will listen to your chest and back to make sure that your breathing seems normal. Early detection can often help with treating respiratory infections and diseases.

doctor. He or she can examine you and perform tests that can determine respiratory issues.

It is absolutely necessary to keep the body's respiratory system in good working order. The body needs it to provide cells with the oxygen they need to function and live. The respiratory system helps the body get rid of waste material that would otherwise poison the cells.

For the most part, breathing is automatic and we do not pay much attention to it until something goes wrong. Some respiratory illness and

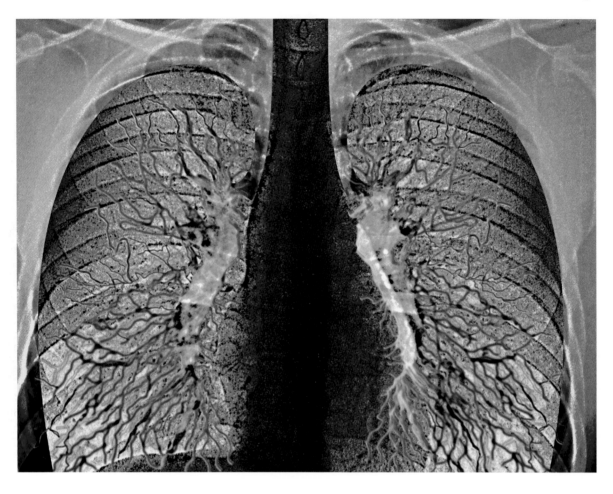

Having a healthy respiratory system is essential to your overall health.

diseases cannot be prevented, but some can. Learning more about your body, practicing healthy habits, and getting regular medical checkups can help keep your respiratory system healthy.

Glossary

alveoli—Tiny, spongy sacs in the lungs where gas exchange takes place.

bronchi—Two branches of the trachea that feed air into the lungs.

capillaries—Small blood vessels in the body. Alveoli are surrounded by blood vessels.

cellular respiration—The cellular process of converting glucose into energy.

cilia—Microscopic hair-like structures that move mucus up and out of the bronchi.

diaphragm—A sheet of strong muscles that changes the volume of the pleural cavity as it contracts and relaxes.

epiglottis—A flap of tissue that covers the opening of the trachea during swallowing.

external respiration—The process of ventilation and the exchange of gases between the lungs and the blood.

glottis—The gap between open vocal cords.

hemoglobin—Protein in red blood cells that carries oxygen to other cells in the body.

intercostals—Muscles between the ribs.

internal respiration—The exchange of gases between the blood and the body's tissues.

larynx—The voice box.

palate—The soft tissue and bone that make up the roof of the mouth.

pharynx—The throat.

pleura—Layers of tissue that protect and cushion the lungs.

septum—The thin piece of tissue in the nose that separates the two nostrils.

spirometer—A medical instrument a doctor or health practitioner uses to measure the lung's airflow.

trachea—The windpipe.

uvula—The cylindrical-shaped piece of tissue that hangs down in the back of the throat.

ventilation—The process of inhalation and exhalation (breathing).

Find Out More

Books

Allman, Toney. *Tuberculosis*. Detroit, MI: Gale Group, 2006.

Barraclough, Sue. *The Respiratory System: Why Am I Out of Breath?*
Chicago, IL: Heinemann Library, 2008.

Bjorklund, Ruth. *Cystic Fibrosis*. New York: Marshall Cavendish
Benchmark, 2008.

Brill, Marlene Targ. *Lung Cancer*. New York: Marshall Cavendish
Benchmark, 2005.

Colligan, L.H. *Sleep Disorders*. New York: Marshall Cavendish
Benchmark, 2008.

Green, Carl. *Nicotine and Tobacco*. Berkeley Heights, NJ: Enslow
Publishers, 2005.

LeVert, Suzanne. *Facts about Nicotine*. New York: Marshall Cavendish
Benchmark, 2006.

Parker, Steve. *Pump It Up: Respiration and Circulation*. Austin, TX:
Raintree Publishers, 2006.

Sanders, Pete. *Smoking*. North Mankato, MN: Stargazer Books, 2006.

Simon, Seymour. *Lungs: Your Respiratory System*. New York, NY:
HarperCollins Publishers, 2007.

Websites

The American Council on Science and Health—The Scoop on Smoking
http://thescooponsmoking.org/index.php

Cystic Fibrosis
http://kidshealth.org/kid/health_problems/heart/cystic_fibrosis.html
. . . .

Inside the Human Body—The Respiratory System
http://www.lung.ca/children/grades7_12/index.html
. . . .

Your Gross and Cool Body: The Respiratory System
http://yucky.discovery.com/flash/body/pg000138.html
. . . .

Your Lungs & Respiratory System
http://www.kidshealth.org/kid/htbw/lungs.html
. . . .

Bibliography

American Council on Science and Health. "The Scoop on Smoking." Accessed June 29, 2008. URL: http://thescooponsmoking.org/xhtml/ effectsHome.php.

American Lung Association. "Childhood Asthma." Accessed June 29, 2008. URL: http://www.lungusa.org/site/pp.asp?c=dvLUK9O0E&b=227 82.

American Lung Association. "How Our Lungs Work." Accessed June 29, 2008. URL: http://www.lungusa.org/site/c.dvLUK9O0E/b.710069/ k.C62F/How_Our_Lungs_Work.htm.

Centers for Disease Control and Prevention. "Questions and Answers About TB." Accessed June 29, 2008. URL: http://www.cdc.gov/tb/faqs/ qa_introduction.htm#Intro1.

Franklin Institute. "Blood Vessels." Accessed June 29, 2008. URL: http:// www.fi.edu/learn/heart/vessels/vessels.html.

Greater Baltimore Medical Center. "Anatomy & Physiology of the Voice." Accessed June 29, 2008. URL: http://www.gbmc.org/voice/ anatomyphysiologyofthelarynx.cfm.

Mayo Foundation for Medical Education and Research. "Bronchitis." Accessed June 29, 2008. URL: http://www.mayoclinic.com/health/ bronchitis/DS00031.

Mayo Foundation for Medical Education and Research. "Sleep Apnea." Accessed June 29, 2008. URL: http://www.mayoclinic.com/health/sleep-apnea/DS00148.

Merck Manuals Online Medical Library. "Acid-Base Balance." Accessed June 29, 2008. URL: http://www.merck.com/mmhe/sec12/ch159/ch159a. html..

National Heart, Lung, and Blood Institute. "What is Cystic Fibrosis?" Accessed June 29, 2008. URL: http://www.nhlbi.nih.gov/health/dci/ Diseases/cf/cf_what.html.

U.S. National Cancer Institute's Surveillance, Epidemiology and End Results (SEER) Program. "Introduction to the Respiratory System." Accessed June 29, 2008. URL: http://training.seer.cancer.gov/module_ anatomy/unit9_1_resp_intro

Index

Page numbers in **boldface** are illustrations and tables.

About the Author

Kristi Lew is the author of more than 20 science books for teachers and young people. Fascinated with science from a young age, she studied biochemistry and genetics in college. Before she started writing full-time, she worked in genetic laboratories for more than 10 years and taught high-school science. When she's not writing, she enjoys sailing with her husband, Simon, aboard their small sailboat, *Proton*. She lives, writes, and sails in St. Petersburg, Florida.